# The Easy Air Fryer Cookbook With Pictures

Simply Delicious, Budget-Friendly Recipes With Step-by-Step Instructions and Stunning Full-Color Photos

**Rosa James**

All images in this cookbook were thoughtfully crafted using AI technology to best represent each recipe as accurately as possible. While every effort has been made to ensure these images reflect the results you can achieve in your kitchen, please note that slight variations may occur based on individual ingredients, tools, and techniques.

We hope these visuals inspire and guide you as you create delicious meals. Enjoy cooking and making these recipes your own!

# Table of Contents

# Introduction

Stuck in the kitchen, scrolling through endless recipes? I know how it feels to crave quick, delicious, and nutritious meals after a busy day. As a mom and passionate cook, I have come to rely on my air fryer as a lifesaver in the kitchen, and I am thrilled to share my favorite recipes with you in ***The Easy Air Fryer Cookbook with Pictures***.

With this cookbook, you will discover how the air fryer can create gourmet-style dishes in a fraction of the time, with minimal effort and no extra oil! Imagine coming home, tossing ingredients together, and in minutes enjoying perfectly crispy chicken tenders, beautifully roasted vegetables, or even indulgent desserts—all guilt-free.

I created this cookbook with busy adults, health-conscious eaters, and culinary enthusiasts in mind. Whether you're whipping up a quick family dinner, exploring healthier eating options, or simply curious to try new food trends, the air fryer is here to make it easy and delicious. Rest assured, there are plenty of delicious vegetarian options included as well. With clear step-by-step instructions and stunning full-color photos, you'll feel confident diving into every recipe.

In my own journey, I have learned that healthy eating does not have to be complicated. With an air fryer, you can reduce unhealthy fats, add variety to your meals, and still enjoy that golden, crispy finish we all love. Most air fryers can bake, roast, and grill too, making it an incredibly versatile tool that cuts down on prep time without sacrificing nutrition.

For the culinary enthusiasts, the air fryer offers a modern twist on traditional recipes and a way to explore new flavors and textures. Imagine hosting a dinner party with perfectly crispy appetizers or transforming weeknight dinners into extraordinary meals that surprise and delight.

This cookbook is not just a collection of recipes; it is a guide to smarter, healthier, and tastier cooking. I have packed these pages with creative, budget-friendly recipes that cater to various dietary preferences and busy schedules. With each dish, you will see how simplicity meets excellence in the kitchen.

So, get ready to dive into a new era of cooking. With this cookbook, delicious, nutritious meals are just moments away, no matter how hectic life gets. Embrace the possibilities of air frying with me, and let us make every meal a delightful, healthy experience.

Warm Regards,
Rosa James x

Chapter 1:

# Breakfast

## *Breakfast Quiche*

**Yield:** 6–8 servings

**Prep:** 10 minutes

**Cook:** 25–30 minutes

**Total:** 35–40 minutes

**Nutritional Information** (per serving):

| **Cals** | **Carbs** | **Fat** | **Protein** | **Fiber** |
|---|---|---|---|---|
| 250 | 12g | 20g | 10g | Negligible |

**Ingredients:**

- 4 x eggs
- 1 cup of heavy cream
- salt and pepper (to taste)
- 1 cup of cheese, shredded
- 1/2 cup of ham, diced
- 1 x pre–made pie crust

**Instructions:**

1. Preheat air fryer to 320°F.
2. In a bowl, whisk together eggs, cream, and salt and pepper to taste.
3. Add cheese and diced ham.
4. Pour mixture into the pie crust.
5. Place in air fryer and cook for 25–30 minutes until set.
6. Let cool slightly before slicing.

## *Cheesy Breakfast Egg Rolls*

**Yield:** 8 egg rolls

**Prep:** 15 minutes

**Cook:** 10 minutes

**Total:** 25 minutes

**Nutritional Information** (per serving):

| Cals | Carbs | Fat | Protein | Fiber |
|---|---|---|---|---|
| 140 | 13g | 7g | 6g | 1g |

**Ingredients:**

- 4 x large eggs
- 1/4 tsp of salt
- 1/4 tsp of pepper
- 1/4 cup of diced bell pepper
- 1/4 cup of diced onion
- 1/2 cup of shredded cheddar cheese
- 1/2 cup of cooked and crumbled breakfast sausage
- 8 x egg roll wrappers
- 1 tbsp of olive oil (for brushing)

**Instructions:**

1. In a medium bowl, whisk together the eggs, salt, and pepper.
2. In a non-stick skillet over medium heat. Add the diced onion and bell pepper, sautéing for about 3–4 minutes until softened.
3. Pour in the beaten eggs and scramble until fully cooked.
4. Remove from heat and stir in the shredded cheese and cooked sausage. Allow to cool slightly.
5. Lay an egg roll wrapper on a clean surface, with one corner pointing toward you (like a diamond shape).
6. Place about 2–3 tablespoons of the egg mixture in the center of the wrapper.
7. Fold the bottom corner over the filling, then fold in the side corners tightly, and roll upwards to seal the egg roll. Use a little water on the edges if necessary to help seal.
8. Preheat your air fryer to 370°F.
9. Lightly brush the egg rolls with olive oil.
10. Place the egg rolls in the air fryer basket in a single layer, making sure they do not touch.
11. Cook for 10 minutes, flipping halfway through, until golden brown and crispy.

## *Oatmeal Cups*

**Yield:** 4 servings

**Prep:** 5 minutes

**Cook:** 15–18 minutes

**Total:** 20–23 minutes

**Nutritional Information** (per serving):

| Cals | Carbs | Fat | Protein | Fiber |
|---|---|---|---|---|
| 180 | 36g | 2g | 4g | 4g |

**Ingredients:**

- 2 cups of rolled oats
- 2 cups of almond milk
- 1/2 cup of honey or maple syrup
- 1 tsp of baking powder
- 1/2 tsp of salt
- fresh fruit (optional, for topping)

**Instructions:**

1. In a bowl, mix all ingredients (minus the fruit) until well combined.
2. Spray 4 silicone muffin cups with cooking spray and fill each cup with the oatmeal mixture.
3. Place the muffin cups in the air fryer basket.
4. Cook at 320°F for 15–18 minutes.
5. Let cool, then top with fresh fruit of your choice if you wish.

## *Apple and Cinnamon Pastries*

**Yield:** 4 servings

**Prep:** 10 minutes

**Cook:** 12–15 minutes

**Total:** 22–25 minutes

**Nutritional Information** (per serving):

| Cals | Carbs | Fat | Protein | Fiber |
|---|---|---|---|---|
| 220 | 28g | 12g | 3g | 1g |

**Ingredients:**

- 1 x sheet of puff pastry
- 1 x apple, peeled and diced
- 2 tbsp of sugar
- 1 tsp of cinnamon
- 1 x egg (for egg wash)

**Instructions:**

1. Preheat the air fryer to 375°F.
2. Mix the diced apple, sugar, and cinnamon in a bowl.
3. Roll out the puff pastry and cut it into 4 squares.
4. Place a tablespoon of the apple mixture in the center of each square, fold, and seal edges.
5. Brush with egg wash.
6. Place pastries in the air fryer and cook for 12–15 minutes until golden brown.

## *Mini Chocolate Chip Pancakes*

**Yield:** 5 servings

**Prep:** 10 minutes

**Cook:** 10–12 minutes

**Total:** 20–22 minutes

**Nutritional Information** (per serving):

| Cals | Carbs | Fat | Protein | Fiber |
|---|---|---|---|---|
| 150 | 25g | 5g | 3g | Negligible |

**Ingredients:**

- 1 packet of pancake mix
- water
- 1/2 cup of chocolate chips
- maple syrup (for serving)

**Instructions:**

1. In a bowl, mix pancake mix with the water as per package directions until smooth.
2. Fold in chocolate chips.
3. Pour batter into 5 greased silicone muffin cups.
4. Place muffin cups in the air fryer basket.
5. Cook at 350°F for 10–12 minutes until cooked through.
6. Serve warm with syrup.

## *Puff Pastry Breakfast Bites*

**Yield:** 12 bites

**Prep:** 15 minutes

**Cook:** 10 minutes

**Total:** 25 minutes

**Nutritional Information** (per serving):

| Cals | Carbs | Fat | Protein | Fiber |
|---|---|---|---|---|
| 120 | 15g | 6g | 2g | 0.5g |

**Ingredients:**

- 1 x sheet puff pastry (thawed if frozen)
- 1/2 cup of fruit jam (such as raspberry, strawberry, or apricot)
- 1 x egg (for egg wash)
- 1 tbsp of water
- powdered sugar (for optional dusting)

**Instructions:**

1. Preheat the air fryer to 375°F.
2. Roll out the puff pastry sheet on a lightly floured surface. Cut it into 3-inch squares (you should get about 12 squares).
3. Place about 1 teaspoon of fruit jam in the center of each puff pastry square (be careful not to overfill, as the jam may leak out during cooking).
4. Fold each square in half diagonally to form a triangle. Press the edges together to seal.
5. Use a fork to crimp the edges for a decorative touch and better sealing.
6. In a small bowl, whisk the egg with the water to create an egg wash.
7. Brush the tops of the sealed pastry triangles with the egg wash.
8. Place the pastry triangles in the air fryer basket in a single layer, making sure they don't touch.
9. Cook for 10 minutes, or until golden brown and puffed up. You may need to do this in batches depending on your air fryer size.
10. Once cooked, remove the pastries from the air fryer and let them cool for a minute.
11. Optionally, dust with powdered sugar before serving.

## Vegetarian Options

### *Spinach and Feta Stuffed Peppers*

**Yield:** 4 servings

**Prep:** 10 minutes

**Cook:** 15 minutes

**Total:** 25 minutes

**Nutritional Information** (per serving):

| Cals | Carbs | Fat | Protein | Fiber |
|---|---|---|---|---|
| 180 | 15g | 10g | 6g | 4g |

**Ingredients:**

- 1 cup of fresh spinach, chopped
- 1/2 cup of feta cheese, crumbled
- 1/4 cup of cooked quinoa
- 1 tbsp of olive oil
- salt and pepper (to taste)
- 2 x bell peppers, halved and seeds removed

**Instructions:**

1. Preheat air fryer to 360°F.
2. In a bowl, mix spinach, feta, quinoa, olive oil, salt, and pepper.
3. Stuff each bell pepper half with the mixture.
4. Place stuffed peppers in the air fryer basket.
5. Cook for 15 minutes until peppers are tender.

## *Avocado Toast*

**Yield:** 2 servings

**Prep:** 5 minutes

**Cook:** 3–5 minutes

**Total:** 8–10 minutes

**Nutritional Information** (per serving):

| Cals | Carbs | Fat | Protein | Fiber |
|---|---|---|---|---|
| 180 | 20g | 10g | 4g | 8g |

**Ingredients:**

- 2 x slices of whole grain bread
- 1 x ripe avocado
- salt and pepper (to taste)
- red pepper flakes
- chili flakes (optional topping)
- cherry tomatoes, halved (optional topping)
- 2 x eggs, poached (optional topping)

**Instructions:**

1. Preheat air fryer to 350°F.
2. Toast bread in the air fryer for 3–5 minutes until golden.
3. Mash avocado in a small bowl and season with salt and pepper.
4. Spread the avocado mixture on toasted bread.
5. Top with red pepper flakes and any optional toppings to serve.
6. Optional: For warm toppings, air fryer again for 1 more minute.

### *Mini Banana Pancakes*

**Yield:** 4 servings

**Prep:** 5 minutes

**Cook:** 8 minutes

**Total:** 13 minutes

**Nutritional Information** (per serving):

| Cals | Carbs | Fat | Protein | Fiber |
|---|---|---|---|---|
| 100 | 20g | 1g | 3g | 2g |

**Ingredients:**

- 1 x ripe banana, mashed
- 1/2 cup of flour
- 1/2 cup of plant-based milk
- 1 tsp of baking powder
- 1/2 tsp of vanilla extract

**Instructions:**

1. Preheat air fryer to 350°F.
2. Combine all of the ingredients in a bowl, mixing until the mixture is smooth.
3. Pour batter into 4 greased silicone muffin cups.
4. Cook for 8 minutes until cooked through.

## *Apple and Cinnamon Oatmeal Bites*

**Yield:** 12 bites

**Prep:** 10 minutes

**Cook:** 15 minutes

**Total:** 25 minutes

**Nutritional Information** (per serving):

| Cals | Carbs | Fat | Protein | Fiber |
|---|---|---|---|---|
| 80 | 17g | 1g | 2g | 2g |

**Ingredients:**

- 2 cups of rolled oats
- 1 cup of applesauce
- 1/2 tsp of cinnamon
- 1/2 cup of diced apples
- 1/4 cup of honey

**Instructions:**

1. Preheat air fryer to 320°F.
2. Mix all of the ingredients in a bowl until well-combined.
3. Spray a mini muffin tin and fill with the mixture (or do so in batches depending on the size of your tin and air fryer).
4. Cook in the air fryer for 15 minutes until set.

Chapter 2:

# Lunch

## *Meatball Sub*

**Yield:** 4 servings

**Prep:** 15 minutes

**Cook:** 12–15 minutes

**Total:** 27 minutes

**Nutritional Information** (per serving):

| Cals | Carbs | Fat | Protein | Fiber |
|---|---|---|---|---|
| 480 | 40g | 22g | 30g | 3g |

**Ingredients:**

- 1 lb of ground beef or turkey
- 1/2 cup of breadcrumbs
- 1/4 cup of grated Parmesan cheese
- 1 x egg
- 2 x cloves garlic, minced
- 1 tsp of Italian seasoning
- salt and pepper (to taste)
- 4 x hoagie rolls
- 1 cup of marinara sauce
- 1 cup of shredded mozzarella cheese

**Instructions:**

1. Preheat your air fryer to 380°F.
2. In a bowl, combine ground meat, breadcrumbs, Parmesan cheese, egg, minced garlic, Italian seasoning, salt, and pepper. Mix until well combined. Form into small meatballs (about 1–1.5 inches in diameter).
3. Place the meatballs in the air fryer basket in a single layer. Cook for about 10–12 minutes until they are browned and cooked through.
4. While the meatballs are cooking, warm the marinara sauce. Once meatballs are done, split the hoagie rolls and place meatballs inside. Top with marinara sauce and mozzarella cheese.
5. Return the assembled subs to the air fryer for an additional 2–3 minutes until the cheese is melted and bubbly.
6. Serve hot!

### *Fried Chicken*

**Yield:** 2 servings

**Prep:** 15 minutes

**Marination:** 1 hour+

**Cook:** 25–30 minutes

**Total:** 1 hour 40–45 minutes+

**Nutritional Information** (per serving):

| Cals | Carbs | Fat | Protein | Fiber |
|---|---|---|---|---|
| 640 | 26g | 36g | 52g | 2g |

**Ingredients:**

- 4 x chicken drumsticks
- 1 cup of buttermilk
- 1 cup of all-purpose flour
- 1 tsp of paprika
- 1 tsp of garlic powder
- 1 tsp of onion powder
- 1 tsp of dried thyme
- 1 tsp of salt
- 1/2 tsp of black pepper
- olive oil spray

**Instructions:**

1. In a bowl, add the chicken pieces and pour in the buttermilk, ensuring they are well coated. Cover and refrigerate for at least 1 hour, or up to overnight for extra flavor.
2. Preheat your air fryer to 380°F.
3. In a shallow bowl, mix together the flour, paprika, garlic powder, onion powder, dried thyme, salt, and black pepper.
4. Remove the marinated chicken from the refrigerator. Shake off excess buttermilk, then dredge each piece in the seasoned flour mixture, pressing lightly to ensure an even coating. Shake off any excess flour.
5. Spray the air fryer basket with cooking spray to prevent sticking. Place the coated chicken pieces in the basket in a single layer, making sure not to overcrowd.
6. Lightly spray the tops of the chicken with cooking spray or olive oil spray.
7. Air fry the chicken for about 25–30 minutes, flipping halfway through the cooking time. The chicken is done when it reaches an internal temperature of 165°F and is golden brown and crispy.
8. Once cooked, remove the chicken from the air fryer and let it rest for a few minutes before serving.

## *Sweet and Sour Pork*

**Yield:** 4 servings

**Prep:** 15 minutes

**Marination:** 30 minutes+

**Cook:** 20 minutes

**Total:** 1 hour 5 minutes+

**Nutritional Information** (per serving):

| Cals | Carbs | Fat | Protein | Fiber |
|---|---|---|---|---|
| 350 | 40g | 10g | 30g | 2g |

**Ingredients:**

Pork

- 1 lb of pork tenderloin, cut into 1-inch cubes
- 1/4 cup of soy sauce
- 1 tbsp of cornstarch
- 1 tbsp of vegetable oil
- 1 x red bell pepper, cut into chunks
- 1 x green bell pepper, cut into chunks
- 1 x onion, cut into chunks
- 1 cup of pineapple chunks (fresh or canned, drained)

Sweet and Sour Sauce

- 1/2 cup of ketchup
- 1/4 cup of apple cider vinegar
- 1/4 cup of brown sugar
- 1 tbsp of soy sauce

**Instructions:**

1. In a bowl, combine the pork cubes with soy sauce, cornstarch, and vegetable oil. Mix well and let the pork marinate for 30 minutes in the refrigerator for extra flavor.
2. Preheat your air fryer to 400°F.
3. In a large bowl, combine the red bell pepper, green bell pepper, onion, and pineapple chunks.
4. In a small bowl, whisk together the ketchup, apple cider vinegar, brown sugar, and soy sauce for the sauce until well combined.
5. In the bowl with the marinated pork, add the mixed vegetables. Stir to combine and ensure everything is coated.

6. Lightly spray the air fryer basket with cooking spray. Place the pork and vegetable mixture in the basket, spreading it out evenly.

7. Cook for 15 minutes, shaking the basket halfway through to ensure even cooking.

8. After 15 minutes, open the air fryer and drizzle the sweet and sour sauce over the pork and vegetables. Toss to coat and cook for an additional 5 minutes.

9. Once cooked, remove from the air fryer and serve warm over rice or on its own.

## *Crispy Chili Beef*

**Yield:** 4 servings

**Prep:** 15 minutes

**Marination:** 30 minutes+

**Cook:** 12–13 minutes

**Total:** 57–58 minutes+

**Nutritional Information** (per serving):

| Cals | Carbs | Fat | Protein | Fiber |
|---|---|---|---|---|
| 280 | 10g | 12g | 30g | 1g |

**Ingredients:**

- 1/4 cup of soy sauce
- 2 x cloves garlic, minced
- 1 tsp of ground ginger
- 1 tbsp of chili paste (adjust to taste)
- 1 tbsp of vegetable oil
- 1 tbsp of sesame oil
- 1 lb of flank steak (or sirloin), thinly sliced against the grain
- 2 tbsp of cornstarch
- sliced green onions (for garnish)
- sesame seeds (for garnish)

**Instructions:**

1. In a bowl, combine soy sauce, minced garlic, ground ginger, chili paste, vegetable oil, and sesame oil. Mix well.
2. Add the sliced beef to the marinade and toss to coat. Cover the bowl and refrigerate for at least 30 minutes for better flavor.
3. After marinating, remove the beef from the refrigerator. Sprinkle cornstarch over the beef slices and toss until all the beef is evenly coated.
4. Preheat your air fryer to 400°F.
5. Place the beef slices in the air fryer basket in a single layer. You may need to do this in batches, depending on the size of your air fryer. Avoid overcrowding to ensure even cooking.
6. Cook for 10 minutes, shaking the basket halfway through to ensure all sides are crispy.

7. Check the beef for doneness. If you like it crispier, you can air fry for an additional 2 –3 minutes.
8. Once cooked, remove the crispy chili beef from the air fryer. Garnish with sliced green onions and sesame seeds.

## *Sour Cream and Chive Jacket Potatoes*

**Yield:** 4 servings

**Prep:** 5 minutes

**Cook:** 35–40 minutes

**Total:** 40–45 minutes

**Nutritional Information** (per serving):

| Cals | Carbs | Fat | Protein | Fiber |
|---|---|---|---|---|
| 200 | 30g | 5g | 6g | 3g |

**Ingredients:**

- 4 x medium-sized russet potatoes
- 2 tbsp of olive oil
- salt and pepper (to taste)
- 1 cup of sour cream
- 1/2 cup of chives

**Instructions:**

1. Scrub the potatoes thoroughly under cold water to remove any dirt. Pat them dry with a paper towel.
2. Using a fork, poke several holes in each potato to allow steam to escape while cooking.
3. Rub each potato with olive oil to coat them evenly. Sprinkle with salt and pepper.
4. Preheat your air fryer to 400°F.
5. Place the potatoes in the air fryer basket, making sure they are not crowded. Cook for about 35–40 minutes, turning them halfway through. Cook until they are crispy on the outside and tender on the inside.
6. Remove the potatoes from the air fryer, slice them open and top with the sour cream before sprinkling the chives across their tops.

## Vegetarian Options

### *Veggie Frittata With Side Salad*

**Yield:** 4 servings

**Prep:** 15 minutes

**Cook:** 15 minutes

**Total:** 30 minutes

**Nutritional Information** (per serving):

| Cals | Carbs | Fat | Protein | Fiber |
|---|---|---|---|---|
| 200 | 5g | 12g | 12g | 2g |

**Ingredients:**

- 1 cup of chopped spinach
- 1/2 cup of diced bell peppers (any color)
- 1/2 cup of diced onion
- 1/2 cup of cherry tomatoes, halved
- 6 x large eggs
- 1/2 cup of plant-based milk
- salt and pepper (to taste)
- 1/2 cup of shredded plant-based hard cheese
- 1 x package of pre-mixed salad

**Instructions:**

1. In a bowl, combine the chopped spinach, bell peppers, onion, and cherry tomatoes. Set aside.
2. In a separate bowl, whisk together the eggs and milk. Season with salt and pepper to taste.
3. Add the prepared vegetable mixture and shredded cheese to the egg mixture. Stir until well combined.
4. Preheat your air fryer to 300°F.
5. Lightly grease an air fryer safe baking dish with cooking spray.
6. Pour the egg and vegetable mixture into the prepared baking dish or skillet.
7. Carefully place the dish in the air fryer basket.
8. Cook for 15 minutes so the frittata sets and a toothpick comes out clean.
9. Arrange your salad.
10. Allow frittata to cool for a few minutes before slicing and serving warm with the salad.

## *Quinoa and Veggie Burgers*

These black bean and quinoa patties are incredibly hearty, and can be topped with whatever toppings your heart desires!

**Yield:** 4 servings

**Prep:** 15 minutes

**Cook:** 12 minutes

**Total:** 27 minutes

**Nutritional Information** (per serving):

| Cals | Carbs | Fat | Protein | Fiber |
| --- | --- | --- | --- | --- |
| 271 | 41g | 6.5g | 12.9g | 7.4g |

**Ingredients:**

- 1/4 cup black beans, drained and rinsed
- 1/2 cup of cooked quinoa
- 1/4 cup grated zucchini (excess moisture squeezed out)
- 1/4 cup diced bell pepper
- 2 tbsp of diced onion
- 1/4 cup of breadcrumbs
- 2 tbsp of grated plant-based hard cheese
- 1 tsp of garlic powder
- 1 tsp of cumin
- 1/2 tsp salt
- 1/4 tsp black pepper
- 1 x egg
- 2 tbsp of plant-based butter
- 4 x whole wheat rolls
- lettuce (optional topping)
- sliced tomatoes (optional topping)
- tomato ketchup (optional topping)

**Instructions:**

1. In a large bowl, mash the black beans using a fork or potato masher, leaving some chunks for texture.
2. Add the cooked quinoa, grated zucchini, diced bell pepper, diced onion, breadcrumbs, cheese, garlic powder, cumin, salt, and pepper to the mashed beans. Mix well.
3. Beat the egg in a separate bowl. Add to the mixture and stir until well combined.

4. With your hands, shape the mixture into patties, roughly 1/2-inch thick. You should have 4 patties.
5. Preheat your air fryer to 375°F.
6. Spray the air fryer basket with cooking spray. Place the patties in a single layer in the basket, ensuring they do not touch.
7. Cook the patties for 12 minutes, flipping them halfway through, until they are golden brown and crispy.
8. Once cooked, carefully remove the patties from the air fryer. Let them cool slightly.
9. Spread butter across the bottom layer of the rolls. Assemble the burgers with optional toppings if desired.

## *Mini Vegetable Pizzas*

**Yield:** 4 servings

**Prep:** 10 minutes

**Cook:** 8–10 minutes

**Total:** 18–20 minutes

**Nutritional Information** (per serving):

| Cals | Carbs | Fat | Protein | Fiber |
|---|---|---|---|---|
| 220 | 30g | 8g | 10g | 3g |

**Ingredients:**

- 4 x small pita bread or naan
- 1/2 cup of pizza sauce (store-bought or homemade)
- 1 cup of shredded plant-based cheese
- 1/2 cup of diced bell peppers
- 1/2 cup of sliced mushrooms
- 1/2 cup of spinach leaves
- 1/4 cup of sliced red onion
- 1 tsp of Italian seasoning
- olive oil spray

**Instructions:**

1. Preheat your air fryer to 370°F.
2. While the air fryer is heating, arrange the pita bread or naan on a clean surface.
3. Evenly spread about 2 tablespoons of pizza sauce on each pita or naan.
4. Sprinkle approximately 1/4 cup of shredded mozzarella cheese on top of the sauce for each mini pizza.
5. Evenly distribute the veggies over the cheese.
6. Sprinkle the Italian seasoning on top.
7. Lightly spray the toppings with olive oil.
8. Place the mini pizzas in the air fryer basket. Depending on your air fryer's size, you might need to work in batches.
9. Cook for 8–10 minutes, so the cheese is melted and bubbly, and the edges are crispy.
10. Let the pizzas cool slightly before serving.

## *Mushrooms on Toast*

**Yield:** 2 servings

**Prep:** 10 minutes

**Cook:** 11–15 minutes

**Total:** 21–25 minutes

**Nutritional Information** (per serving):

| Cals | Carbs | Fat | Protein | Fiber |
|---|---|---|---|---|
| 280 | 36g | 12g | 9g | 5g |

**Ingredients:**

- 8 oz of button mushrooms, sliced
- 1 tablespoon of olive oil
- 2 cloves garlic, minced
- 1 teaspoon of dried thyme
- salt and pepper (to taste)
- 4 x slices of whole-grain bread
- 1/4 cup of vegan cream cheese
- fresh parsley (for garnish)

**Instructions:**

1. In a bowl, combine the sliced mushrooms, olive oil, minced garlic, dried thyme, salt, and pepper. Toss to coat the mushrooms evenly.
2. Preheat your air fryer to 375°F.
3. Place the seasoned mushrooms in the air fryer basket in a single layer. In batches if necessary.
4. Air fry for 8–10 minutes, shaking the basket halfway through, until the mushrooms are tender and browned.
5. Toast the bread for 3–5 minutes, depending on how crispy you like it.
6. Spread cream cheese on each slice of toasted bread.
7. Top each slice with the cooked mushrooms.
8. Garnish with fresh parsley. Serve immediately while warm.

## *Tomato Basil Soup*

**Yield:** 4 servings

**Prep:** 10 minutes

**Cook:** 20 minutes

**Total:** 30 minutes

**Nutritional Information** (per serving):

| Cals | Carbs | Fat | Protein | Fiber |
|---|---|---|---|---|
| 120 | 12g | 7g | 3g | 3g |

**Ingredients:**

- 6 x medium ripe tomatoes, quartered
- 1 x red onion, chopped
- 4 x cloves garlic, peeled
- 2 tbsp of olive oil
- salt and pepper (to taste)
- 1 tsp of dried basil
- 3 cups of vegetable broth
- fresh basil leaves (for garnish)

**Instructions:**

1. Preheat the air fryer to 375°F.
2. In a large bowl, toss the quartered tomatoes, chopped red onion, and garlic cloves with olive oil, salt, pepper, and dried basil until well coated.
3. Place the mixture in the air fryer basket in a single layer (you may need to do this in batches).
4. Air fry for 15–20 minutes, shaking the basket halfway through, until the vegetables are roasted and caramelized.
5. Transfer the roasted vegetables to a blender. Add the vegetable broth and blend until smooth. Adjust seasoning if needed.
6. Pour the blended soup into a pot and heat over medium heat for about 5 minutes, stirring occasionally.
7. Divide the soup among bowls and garnish with fresh basil leaves. Serve warm.

Chapter 3:

# Dinner

## *Beef Tacos*

**Yield:** 6 servings

**Prep:** 10 minutes

**Cook:** 15 minutes

**Total:** 25 minutes

**Nutritional Information** (per serving):

| Cals | Carbs | Fat | Protein | Fiber |
|---|---|---|---|---|
| 250 | 2–3g | 15g | 20g | 1g |

**Ingredients:**

- 1 lb of ground beef
- 1 tbsp of taco seasoning
- 6 x taco shells
- Toppings: cheese, lettuce, tomato, salsa

**Instructions:**

1. Preheat the air fryer to 400°F.
2. In a skillet, brown the ground beef over medium heat; drain excess fat.
3. Mix in taco seasoning, cooking for another 2 minutes.
4. Place taco shells in the air fryer basket and fill each with beef.
5. Air fry for 5 minutes to warm the shells.
6. Remove and top with desired toppings.

## *Whole Grain Turkey Burgers*

**Yield:** 4 servings

**Prep:** 10 minutes

**Cook:** 15 minutes

**Total:** 25 minutes

**Nutritional Information** (per serving):

| Cals | Carbs | Fat | Protein | Fiber |
|---|---|---|---|---|
| 290 | 12.5g | 15g | 26g | 3g |

**Ingredients:**

- 1 lb of ground turkey
- 1 tsp of garlic powder
- 1 tsp of onion powder
- salt and pepper (to taste)
- 4 tbsp of unsalted butter, softened
- 4 x whole grain burger buns
- your favorite toppings and condiments (optional)

**Instructions:**

1. Preheat the air fryer to 375°F.
2. In a bowl, combine ground turkey, garlic powder, onion powder, salt, and pepper.
3. Form into 4 patties using your hands.
4. Place the patties in the air fryer basket.
5. Cook for 15 minutes, flipping halfway through, until internal temperature reaches 165°F.
6. Spread the butter across the whole grain buns, then top with your favorite toppings and condiments.

## *Honey Garlic Shrimp*

**Yield:** 4 servings

**Prep:** 15 minutes

**Cook:** 8 minutes

**Total:** 23 minutes

**Nutritional Information** (per serving):

| Cals | Carbs | Fat | Protein | Fiber |
|---|---|---|---|---|
| 250 | 9g | 8g | 24g | Negligible |

**Ingredients:**

- 2 tbsp of honey
- 2 tbsp of soy sauce
- 1 tsp of garlic, minced
- 1 tbsp of olive oil
- 1 lb of shrimp, peeled and deveined

**Instructions:**

1. Preheat the air fryer to 400°F.
2. In a bowl, mix honey, soy sauce, garlic, and olive oil.
3. Toss shrimp in the marinade until well coated.
4. Place the shrimp in the air fryer basket in a single layer.
5. Cook for 8 minutes, shaking the basket halfway through.
6. Serve hot!

### *Chicken and Broccoli*

**Yield:** 4 servings

**Prep:** 10 minutes

**Cook:** 20 minutes

**Total:** 30 minutes

**Nutritional Information** (per serving):

| Cals | Carbs | Fat | Protein | Fiber |
|---|---|---|---|---|
| 320 | 10g | 10g | 40g | 4g |

**Ingredients:**

- 1 lb of chicken breast, cubed
- 2 cups of broccoli florets
- 2 tbsp of soy sauce
- 1 tbsp of olive oil
- 1 tsp of garlic powder
- salt and pepper (to taste)
- sesame seeds (for garnish)

**Instructions:**

1. Preheat the air fryer to 380°F.
2. In a bowl, combine the cubed chicken, soy sauce, olive oil, garlic powder, salt, and pepper.
3. Toss until the chicken is well coated.
4. Add the broccoli florets to the bowl and mix gently.
5. Place the chicken and broccoli mixture in the air fryer basket.
6. Cook for 20 minutes, shaking the basket halfway through for even cooking.
7. Garnish with sesame seeds before serving.

*Seafood Delights*

**Yield:** 4 servings

**Prep:** 15 minutes

**Cook:** 10 minutes

**Total:** 25 minutes

**Nutritional Information** (per serving):

| Cals | Carbs | Fat | Protein | Fiber |
|---|---|---|---|---|
| 320 | 15g | 18g | 25g | Negligible |

**Ingredients:**

- 1 lb of shrimp, peeled and deveined
- 1 lb of crab cakes
- 1 tbsp of olive oil
- 1 tsp of garlic powder
- salt and pepper (to taste)
- lemon wedges (for serving)

**Instructions:**

1. Preheat the air fryer to 400°F.
2. In a bowl, toss shrimp with olive oil, garlic powder, salt, and pepper.
3. Place the crab cakes and seasoned shrimp in the air fryer basket.
4. Cook for 10 minutes, shaking the basket halfway through.
5. Serve with lemon wedges.

### *Butternut Squash and Carrot Soup*

**Yield:** 4 servings

**Prep:** 10 minutes

**Cook:** 20 minutes

**Total:** 30 minutes

**Nutritional Information** (per serving):

| Cals | Carbs | Fat | Protein | Fiber |
|---|---|---|---|---|
| 150 | 24g | 6g | 4g | 5g |

**Ingredients:**

- 1 x medium butternut squash, peeled, seeded, and diced
- 2 x large carrots, peeled and sliced
- 1 x onion, chopped
- 3 x cloves garlic, peeled
- 2 tbsp of olive oil
- 4 cups of vegetable broth
- 1 tsp of ground cumin
- salt and pepper (to taste)
- fresh cilantro (for optional garnish)

**Instructions:**

1. Preheat the air fryer to 375°F.
2. In a large bowl, toss the diced butternut squash, sliced carrots, onion, and garlic with olive oil, cumin, salt, and pepper until well coated.
3. Place the vegetable mixture in the air fryer basket in a single layer (you may need to do this in batches). Air fry for 15–20 minutes, shaking the basket halfway through, until the vegetables are tender and slightly caramelized.
4. Transfer the roasted vegetables to a blender. Add vegetable broth and blend until smooth. Adjust seasoning if needed.
5. Pour the blended soup into a pot and heat over medium heat for about 5 minutes, stirring occasionally.
6. Divide the soup among bowls and garnish with fresh cilantro if desired. Serve warm.

## Vegetarian Options

### *Chipotle Peppers and Gnocchi*

**Yield:** 4 servings

**Prep:** 10 minutes

**Cook:** 15 minutes

**Total:** 25 minutes

**Nutritional Information** (per serving):

| Cals | Carbs | Fat | Protein | Fiber |
|---|---|---|---|---|
| 380 | 58g | 14g | 10g | 4g |

**Ingredients:**

- 16 oz of potato gnocchi (frozen)
- 1 tbsp of olive oil
- 1 tsp of garlic powder
- 1 tsp of smoked paprika
- salt (to taste)
- 1 x can (7 oz) of chipotle peppers in adobo sauce
- 1 cup of cherry tomatoes, halved
- 1/2 cup of corn
- 1/4 cup of fresh cilantro, chopped (for garnish)
- juice of 1 lime
- 1/4 cup of grated parmesan cheese (optional)

**Instructions:**

1. In a large bowl, combine gnocchi, olive oil, garlic powder, smoked paprika, and salt. Toss to coat evenly.
2. Preheat the air fryer to 400°F.
3. Place the seasoned gnocchi in the air fryer basket in a single layer.
4. Cook for 10–12 minutes, shaking the basket halfway through, until the gnocchi is golden and crispy.
5. While the gnocchi cooks, in a separate bowl, add the chipotle peppers along with a few spoonsful of the adobo sauce (or more, depending on desired spice level).
6. Mix in the halved cherry tomatoes and corn, stirring until well combined.
7. Once the gnocchi is crispy, add it to the bowl with the chipotle mixture. Toss gently to combine everything.

8. Return the mixture to the air fryer for an additional 2 –3 minutes to heat through, if necessary.
9. Squeeze fresh lime juice over the mixture.
10. Plate and garnish with chopped cilantro and grated parmesan cheese, if desired.

## *Crispy Tofu Over Noodles*

**Yield:** 4 servings

**Prep:** 20 minutes

**Cook:** 23–26 minutes

**Total:** 43–46 minutes

**Nutritional Information** (per serving):

| Cals | Carbs | Fat | Protein | Fiber |
|---|---|---|---|---|
| 340 | 50g | 12g | 18g | 4g |

**Ingredients:**

- 8 oz of rice noodles
- 1 block (14 oz) of firm tofu, drained and pressed
- 3 tbsp of soy sauce
- 1 tbsp of sesame oil
- 1 tbsp of cornstarch
- 1 tbsp of olive oil
- 2 x cloves garlic, minced
- 1 tbsp of fresh ginger, grated
- 1 cup of broccoli florets
- 1 x red bell pepper, sliced
- 1 x carrot, julienned
- 2 x green onions, sliced (for garnish)
- sesame seeds (for garnish)

**Ingredients:**

1. Cook the noodles according to package instructions. Drain, rinse with cold water, and set aside.
2. Cut the tofu into cubes and place in a bowl. Add 2 tablespoons of soy sauce and the sesame oil to the tofu. Toss gently to coat. Sprinkle cornstarch over the tofu and toss again until evenly coated.
3. Preheat the air fryer to 375°F.
4. Place the tofu cubes in a single layer in the air fryer basket. Cook for 15 minutes, shaking the basket halfway through until the tofu is golden brown and crispy.
5. While the tofu is cooking, heat olive oil in a large skillet or wok over medium heat.

6. Add minced garlic and grated ginger, sautéing for about 1 minute until fragrant.
7. Add broccoli, bell pepper, and carrot. Stir-fry for about 5 –7 minutes, until vegetables are tender-crisp.
8. Once the tofu is cooked, add the cooked noodles to the skillet with the sautéed vegetables.
9. Pour in the remaining soy sauce and toss everything together. Stir-fry for an additional 2–3 minutes until everything is heated through and well-combined.
10. Plate the noodles and top with crispy tofu. Garnish with sliced green onions and sesame seeds before serving.

## *Mushroom Burgers With Fries*

**Yield:** 4 servings

**Prep:** 10 minutes

**Cook:** 15 minutes

**Total:** 25 minutes

**Nutritional Information** (per serving):

| Cals | Carbs | Fat | Protein | Fiber |
|---|---|---|---|---|
| 364 | 42g | 19g | 8g | 3g |

**Ingredients:**

- 1/2 cup of breadcrumbs
- 1/4 cup of grated cheese
- 1 tsp of garlic powder
- salt and pepper (to taste)
- 4 x large portobello mushrooms
- 1 lb of frozen fries
- 4 tbsp of unsalted butter, softened
- 4 x white burger buns

**Instructions:**

1. Preheat air fryer to 350°F.
2. Mix breadcrumbs, cheese, garlic powder, salt, and pepper in a bowl.
3. Remove the stems from the mushrooms.
4. Stuff each mushroom cap with the bread crumb mixture.
5. Place in air fryer basket and cook for 15 minutes.
6. Add the fries to the basket for the final 10 minutes.
7. Spread the butter across 1 half of the burger buns.
8. Sandwich the mushrooms in the buns and serve with a portion of the fries.

***Sweet Potato and Black Bean Tacos***

**Yield:** 4 servings

**Prep:** 15 minutes

**Cook:** 20 minutes

**Total:** 35 minutes

**Nutritional Information** (per serving):

| Cals | Carbs | Fat | Protein | Fiber |
|---|---|---|---|---|
| 360 | 60g | 8g | 10g | 12g |

**Ingredients:**

- 2 x large sweet potatoes, peeled and diced
- 1 x can (15 oz) of black beans, rinsed and drained
- 1 tsp of cumin
- 1 tsp of chili powder
- salt and pepper (to taste)
- 8 x corn tortillas
- Optional toppings: avocado, salsa, cilantro

**Instructions:**

1. Preheat the air fryer to 400°F.
2. In a bowl, combine diced sweet potatoes, black beans, cumin, chili powder, salt, and pepper.
3. Place the mixture in the air fryer basket in a single layer.
4. Cook for 20 minutes, shaking halfway through.
5. Warm the corn tortillas in the air fryer for the last 2 minutes.
6. Assemble tacos with the sweet potato-black bean mix and desired toppings.

## *Spinach and Feta Stuffed Mushrooms With Sweet Potato Fries*

**Yield:** 4 servings

**Prep:** 10 minutes

**Cook:** 15 minutes

**Total:** 25 minutes

**Nutritional Information** (per serving):

| Cals | Carbs | Fat | Protein | Fiber |
|---|---|---|---|---|
| 225 | 21g | 17.5g | 5.5g | 2g |

**Ingredients:**

- 1 cup of fresh spinach, chopped
- 1/2 cup of feta cheese, crumbled
- 1/4 cup of cream cheese, softened
- 1 x clove garlic, minced
- salt and pepper (to taste)
- 4 x large portobello mushrooms, stems removed
- 1 tbsp of olive oil
- 1 lb of frozen sweet potato fries

**Instructions:**

1. Preheat the air fryer to 375°F.
2. In a bowl, mix spinach, feta, cream cheese, garlic, salt, and pepper.
3. Brush portobello mushrooms with olive oil and fill each with the mixture.
4. Place in the air fryer basket and cook for 15 minutes.
5. Add the sweet potato fries to the basket for the final 10 minutes.
6. Serve hot together.

Chapter 4:

# Snacks and Sides

### *Turkey Meatballs*

**Yield:** 4 servings

**Prep:** 10 minutes

**Cook:** 15–20 minutes

**Total:** 25–30 minutes

**Nutritional Information** (per serving):

| Cals | Carbs | Fat | Protein | Fiber |
|---|---|---|---|---|
| 300 | 10g | 18g | 28g | Negligible |

**Ingredients:**

- 1 lb of ground turkey
- 1/4 cup of breadcrumbs
- 1/4 cup of grated Parmesan cheese
- 1 x egg
- 1 tsp of garlic powder
- salt and pepper (to taste)

**Instructions:**

1. In a bowl, combine ground meat, breadcrumbs, Parmesan, egg, garlic powder, salt, and pepper.
2. Preheat the air fryer to 375°F.
3. Roll mixture into 1-inch meatballs in your hands.
4. Arrange the meatballs in the basket in a single layer.
5. Cook for 15–20 minutes, shaking the basket halfway.

## *Bacon-Wrapped Jalapeño Poppers*

**Yield:** 4 servings

**Prep:** 5 minutes

**Cook:** 15 minutes

**Total:** 20 minutes

**Nutritional Information** (per serving):

| Cals | Carbs | Fat | Protein | Fiber |
|---|---|---|---|---|
| 220 | 4g | 18g | 10g | 1g |

**Ingredients:**

- 8 x jalapeños, halved and seeded
- 4 oz of cream cheese, softened
- 8 x strips of bacon, cut in half

**Instructions:**

1. Preheat the air fryer to 400°F.
2. Fill each jalapeño half with cream cheese.
3. Wrap each stuffed jalapeño with half a strip of bacon.
4. Place the poppers in the air fryer in a single layer and cook for 15 minutes.

## *Chicken Tenders*

**Yield:** 4 servings

**Prep:** 5 minutes

**Cook:** 12–15 minutes

**Total:** 17–20 minutes

**Nutritional Information** (per serving):

| Cals | Carbs | Fat | Protein | Fiber |
|---|---|---|---|---|
| 350 | 30g | 10g | 30g | 1g |

**Ingredients:**

- 1 lb of chicken breast, cut into strips
- 1 cup of breadcrumbs
- 1 tsp of paprika
- 1/2 tsp of garlic powder
- 1 x egg, beaten
- salt and pepper (to taste)

**Instructions:**

1. Preheat air fryer to 400°F.
2. In one bowl, mix breadcrumbs, paprika, garlic powder, salt, and pepper. In another bowl, place beaten egg.
3. Dip chicken strips into egg then coat with the breadcrumb mixture.
4. Arrange tenders in the air fryer and cook for 12–15 minutes, flipping halfway.

## *Sausage Balls*

**Yield:** 4 servings

**Prep:** 5 minutes

**Cook:** 15–20 minutes

**Total:** 20–25 minutes

**Nutritional Information** (per serving):

| Cals | Carbs | Fat | Protein | Fiber |
|---|---|---|---|---|
| 350 | 6g | 28g | 24g | Negligible |

**Ingredients:**

- 1 lb of breakfast sausage
- 1 cup of cheddar cheese, shredded
- 1 cup of biscuit mix

**Instructions:**

1. Preheat air fryer to 375°F.
2. In a bowl, mix sausage, cheese, and biscuit mix until combined.
3. Form mixture into small balls and place in the air fryer basket.
4. Cook for 15–20 minutes until golden brown.

## *Popcorn Chicken*

**Yield:** 4 servings

**Prep:** 20 minutes

**Cook:** 10–12 minutes

**Total:** 30–32 minutes

**Nutritional Information** (per serving):

| Cals | Carbs | Fat | Protein | Fiber |
|---|---|---|---|---|
| 330 | 30g | 10g | 30g | 1g |

**Ingredients:**

- 1 lb of chicken breast, cut into bite-sized pieces
- 1 cup of buttermilk
- 1 cup of breadcrumbs
- 1 tsp of garlic powder
- salt and pepper (to taste)

**Instructions:**

1. Preheat air fryer to 400°F.
2. Soak chicken pieces in buttermilk for 15 minutes.
3. Combine breadcrumbs, garlic powder, salt, and pepper in a bowl.
4. Coat each chicken piece in the breadcrumb mixture.
5. Arrange in a single layer in the air fryer basket.
6. Cook for 10–12 minutes, shaking halfway through.

## *Corn on the Cob*

**Yield:** 2 servings

**Prep:** 1 minute

**Cook:** 12–15 minutes

**Total:** 13–16 minutes

**Nutritional Information** (per serving):

| Cals | Carbs | Fat | Protein | Fiber |
|---|---|---|---|---|
| 70 | 16g | 1.7g | 2.5g | 2g |

**Ingredients:**

- 2 x ears of corn, husked
- 1 tbsp of butter, melted
- salt (to taste)

**Instructions:**

1. Brush corn with melted butter and sprinkle with salt.
2. Preheat air fryer to 400°F.
3. Place corn in the basket and cook for 12–15 minutes, turning halfway.

### *Sweet Potato Fries*

**Yield:** 4 servings

**Prep:** 10 minutes

**Cook:** 20 minutes

**Total:** 30 minutes

**Nutritional Information** (per serving):

| Cals | Carbs | Fat | Protein | Fiber |
|---|---|---|---|---|
| 180 | 30g | 7g | 2g | 4g |

**Ingredients:**

- 2 x medium sweet potatoes, cut into fries
- 1 tbsp of olive oil
- 1/2 tsp of paprika
- salt and pepper (to taste)

**Instructions:**

1. Preheat air fryer to 400°F.
2. Toss sweet potatoes with olive oil, paprika, salt, and pepper.
3. Place in the air fryer basket and cook for 20 minutes, shaking halfway.

## Vegetarian Options

### *Cauliflower Bites*

**Yield:** 4 servings

**Prep:** 10 minutes

**Cook:** 15 minutes

**Total:** 25 minutes

**Nutritional Information** (per serving):

| Cals | Carbs | Fat | Protein | Fiber |
|---|---|---|---|---|
| 150 | 17g | 7g | 7g | 5g |

**Ingredients:**

- 1 cup of breadcrumbs
- 1/2 cup of grated Parmesan cheese
- 1 tsp of garlic powder
- 1 tsp of paprika
- salt (to taste)
- 1 x head cauliflower, cut into florets
- 2 x eggs, beaten

**Instructions:**

1. Preheat air fryer to 375°F.
2. In a bowl, mix breadcrumbs, Parmesan, garlic powder, paprika, and salt.
3. Dip cauliflower florets in egg, then coat with the bread crumb mixture.
4. Place in the air fryer basket and cook for 15 minutes until crispy.

### *Roasted Brussels Sprouts*

**Yield:** 4 servings

**Prep:** 10 minutes

**Cook:** 15 minutes

**Total:** 25 minutes

**Nutritional Information** (per serving):

| Cals | Carbs | Fat | Protein | Fiber |
|---|---|---|---|---|
| 120 | 12g | 8g | 4g | 4g |

**Ingredients:**

- 1 lb of Brussels sprouts, halved
- 2 tbsp of olive oil
- salt and pepper (to taste)
- 1 tsp of balsamic vinegar

**Instructions:**

1. Preheat air fryer to 375°F.
2. Toss Brussels sprouts with olive oil, salt, and pepper.
3. Place in air fryer basket and cook for 15 minutes until crispy.
4. Drizzle with balsamic vinegar before serving.

## *Zucchini Chips*

**Yield:** 4 servings

**Prep:** 10 minutes

**Cook:** 10 minutes

**Total:** 20 minutes

**Nutritional Information** (per serving):

| Cals | Carbs | Fat | Protein | Fiber |
|---|---|---|---|---|
| 100 | 13g | 5g | 3g | 3g |

**Ingredients:**

- 2 x medium zucchinis, thinly sliced
- 1 tbsp of olive oil
- 1/2 cup of breadcrumbs
- salt and pepper (to taste)

**Instructions:**

1. Preheat air fryer to 375°F.
2. Toss zucchini slices with olive oil, salt, and pepper.
3. Coat with breadcrumbs.
4. Place in the air fryer basket and cook for 10 minutes, flipping halfway.

## *Crispy Chickpeas*

**Yield:** 4 servings

**Prep:** 5 minutes

**Cook:** 15 minutes

**Total:** 20 minutes

**Nutritional Information** (per serving):

| Cals | Carbs | Fat | Protein | Fiber |
|---|---|---|---|---|
| 120 | 20g | 4g | 6g | 6g |

**Ingredients:**

- 1 x can (15 oz) of chickpeas, rinsed and drained
- 1 tbsp of olive oil
- 1 tsp of garlic powder
- 1 tsp of paprika
- salt (to taste)

**Instructions:**

1. Preheat the air fryer to 400°F.
2. Pat chickpeas dry with a paper towel.
3. In a bowl, toss chickpeas with olive oil, garlic powder, paprika, and salt.
4. Place in the air fryer basket in a single layer.
5. Cook for 15 minutes, shaking the basket halfway through.

### *Beet Chips*

**Yield:** 4 servings

**Prep:** 5 minutes

**Cook:** 25 minutes

**Total:** 30 minutes

**Nutritional Information** (per serving):

| Cals | Carbs | Fat | Protein | Fiber |
|---|---|---|---|---|
| 90 | 3g | 4.5g | Negligible | 3g |

**Ingredients:**

- 2 medium beets, thinly sliced
- 1 tbsp of olive oil
- salt (to taste)

**Instructions:**

1. Toss beet slices in olive oil and salt.
2. Preheat air fryer to 350°F.
3. Place beet slices in a single layer in the basket.
4. Cook for 25 minutes until crispy, flipping halfway.

### *Asparagus*

**Yield:** 4 servings

**Prep:** 5 minutes

**Cook:** 7–10 minutes

**Total:** 12–15 minutes

**Nutritional Information** (per serving):

| Cals | Carbs | Fat | Protein | Fiber |
|---|---|---|---|---|
| 50 | 5g | 3.5g | 1g | 3g |

**Ingredients:**

- 1 lb of asparagus, trimmed
- 1 tbsp of olive oil
- salt and pepper (to taste)

**Instructions:**

1. Toss asparagus with olive oil, salt, and pepper.
2. Preheat air fryer to 400°F.
3. Cook asparagus for 7–10 minutes until tender.

Chapter 5:

# Desserts

## *Peach Cobbler*

**Yield:** 4 servings

**Prep:** 10 minutes

**Cook:** 20 minutes

**Total:** 30 minutes

**Nutritional Information** (per serving):

| Cals | Carbs | Fat | Protein | Fiber |
|---|---|---|---|---|
| 220 | 36g | 8g | 3g | 2g |

**Ingredients:**

- 4 x ripe peaches, sliced
- 1/2 cup of sugar
- 1 tsp of cinnamon
- 1 cup of biscuit mix
- 1/2 cup of milk
- 1/4 cup of butter, melted

**Instructions:**

1. Toss peach slices with sugar and cinnamon in a bowl, then place an air fryer silicone tray and pop it in the air fryer.
2. In another bowl, mix biscuit mix, milk, and melted butter until smooth.
3. Pour batter over the peaches in the air fryer.
4. Set to 350°F and air fry for 20 minutes.

## *Red Velvet Cake*

**Yield:** 12 servings

**Prep:** 15 minutes

**Cook:** 25 minutes

**Total:** 40 minutes

**Nutritional Information** (per serving):

| Cals | Carbs | Fat | Protein | Fiber |
|---|---|---|---|---|
| 220 | 30g | 10g | 3g | 1g |

**Ingredients:**

- 1 1/2 cups of all-purpose flour
- 1 cup of sugar
- 1 tsp of cocoa powder
- 1 tsp of baking soda
- 1/2 tsp of salt
- 1 cup of vegetable oil
- 1 cup of buttermilk
- 2 x large eggs
- 1 tbsp of red food coloring
- 1 tsp of vanilla extract

**Instructions:**

1. In a bowl, mix flour, sugar, cocoa powder, baking soda, and salt.
2. In another bowl, mix oil, buttermilk, eggs, food coloring, and vanilla.
3. Combine wet and dry ingredients until smooth.
4. Preheat air fryer to 320°F.
5. Pour batter into an air fryer safe greased baking pan and air fry for 25 minutes.

## *Chocolate Lava Cakes*

**Yield:** 4 servings

**Prep:** 10 minutes

**Cook:** 12 minutes

**Total:** 22 minutes

**Nutritional Information** (per serving):

| Cals | Carbs | Fat | Protein | Fiber |
|---|---|---|---|---|
| 380 | 30g | 28g | 6g | 1g |

**Ingredients:**

Cakes

- 1/2 cup (1 stick) of unsalted butter
- 1 cup of semi-sweet chocolate chips
- 2 x large eggs
- 2 x large egg yolks
- 1/4 cup of granulated sugar
- a pinch of salt
- 2 tbsp of all-purpose flour
- 1 tsp of vanilla extract

Topping

- 1 cup of heavy whipping cream
- 2 tbsp of powdered sugar
- 1 tsp of vanilla extract
- 1 cup of sliced strawberries
- additional powdered sugar for dusting

**Instructions:**

1. Grease four 6-ounce ramekins with butter or cooking spray and dust with cocoa powder. Set aside.
2. In a microwave-safe bowl, combine the unsalted butter and semi-sweet chocolate chips. Microwave in 30-second intervals, stirring in between, until completely melted and smooth.
3. In a separate mixing bowl, whisk together eggs, egg yolks, granulated sugar, and a pinch of salt until well combined.

4. Gradually pour the melted chocolate mixture into the egg mixture, whisking continuously.
5. Stir in the flour and vanilla extract until just combined. Do not overmix.
6. Pour the batter evenly into the prepared ramekins, filling each only about 3/4 full.
7. Preheat your air fryer to 350°F.
8. Place the filled ramekins in the air fryer basket. Cook for 10 –12 minutes, or until the edges look set but the center is still soft.
9. While the cakes are cooking, whip the heavy cream, powdered sugar, and vanilla extract in a mixing bowl until soft peaks form.
10. Once done, remove the ramekins from the air fryer and let them cool for a minute. Then, carefully run a knife around the edges and invert onto plates.
11. Top each lava cake with a generous dollop of whipped cream, sliced strawberries, and a dusting of powdered sugar.

## *Pumpkin Muffins*

**Yield:** 12 muffins

**Prep:** 10 minutes

**Cook:** 15 minutes

**Total:** 25 minutes

**Nutritional Information** (per muffin):

| Cals | Carbs | Fat | Protein | Fiber |
|---|---|---|---|---|
| 110 | 18g | 4g | 2g | 1g |

**Ingredients:**

- 1 cup of pumpkin puree
- 1 1/2 cups of all-purpose flour
- 1/2 cup of sugar
- 1/4 cup of vegetable oil
- 2 x large eggs
- 1 tsp of baking soda
- 1 tsp of cinnamon
- 1/2 tsp of salt

**Instructions:**

1. In a bowl, mix pumpkin puree, sugar, oil, and eggs.
2. In another bowl, combine flour, baking soda, cinnamon, and salt.
3. Gradually mix dry ingredients into wet.
4. Preheat air fryer to 320°F and pour batter into silicone air fryer muffin cups.
5. Air fry for 15 minutes.

## *Charred Fruit Skewers*

**Yield:** 4 servings

**Prep:** 10 minutes

**Cook:** 5 minutes

**Total:** 15 minutes

**Nutritional Information** (per skewer):

| Cals | Carbs | Fat | Protein | Fiber |
|---|---|---|---|---|
| 80 | 21g | Negligible | 1g | 2g |

**Ingredients:**

- 1 cup of pineapple chunks
- 1 cup of strawberries, hulled
- 1 cup of banana slices
- 2 tbsp of honey
- 4 x small skewers

**Instructions:**

1. Preheat air fryer to 350°F.
2. Thread the fruit onto four skewers evenly.
3. Brush the skewers with honey if desired.
4. Air fry for 5 minutes until slightly charred and the banana is caramelized.

## *Berry Crumble*

**Yield:** 4 servings

**Prep:** 15 minutes

**Cook:** 20 minutes

**Total:** 35 minutes

**Nutritional Information** (per serving):

| **Cals** | **Carbs** | **Fat** | **Protein** | **Fiber** |
|---|---|---|---|---|
| 240 | 38g | 8g | 3g | 5g |

**Ingredients:**

Filling

- 2 cups of mixed berries (blackberries, blueberries, raspberries)
- 1/4 cup of granulated sugar (adjust based on the sweetness of berries)
- 1 tbsp of lemon juice
- 1 tbsp of cornstarch
- 1 tsp of vanilla extract

Topping

- 1 cup of rolled oats
- 1/2 cup of all-purpose flour
- 1/4 cup of brown sugar
- 1/4 tsp of salt
- 1/2 tsp of ground cinnamon
- 1/4 cup of cold unsalted butter, cubed

**Instructions:**

1. In a mixing bowl, combine the mixed berries, granulated sugar, lemon juice, cornstarch, and vanilla extract. Toss gently to coat the berries evenly. Set aside.
2. In a separate bowl, mix the rolled oats, flour, brown sugar, salt, and ground cinnamon.
3. Add the cold cubed butter to the dry ingredients and use your fingers or a pastry cutter to mix until the mixture resembles coarse crumbs.
4. Lightly grease a baking dish that fits in your air fryer.
5. Pour the berry mixture into the bottom of the dish.

6. Evenly sprinkle the crumble topping over the berry filling.
7. Preheat your air fryer to 320°F.
8. Place the baking dish in the air fryer basket.
9. Cook for 15–20 minutes or until the topping is golden brown and the berries are bubbling.
10. Carefully remove the baking dish from the air fryer and allow it to cool for a few minutes.
11. Garnish with additional fresh blackberries, blueberries, and raspberries before serving.

Chapter 6:

# Coffee Time With Rosa: Before You Go – Air Fryer Troubleshooting, Maintenance, Tips, and FAQs

We may be nearing the end of our journey, but there's still time for one last chat! Before you dive into your air frying adventures, let's take a moment to revisit the essentials. In this chapter, we'll troubleshoot common issues, answer frequently asked questions, and share some valuable tips, tricks, and maintenance advice to ensure you're set up for success.

Think of this as your final guide to mastering your new kitchen companion—everything you need before you take the next step in your air frying journey!

## Frequently Asked Questions (FAQs) That Beginners Often Have About Cooking With an Air Fryer:

### *1. What Are the Basic Safety Measures to Consider When Using an Air Fryer?*

Always confirm that your hands are dry before handling the air fryer. Do not fill the cooking basket more than two-thirds full to avoid food spillage that could cause smoke or a fire hazard.

### *2. How Often Should I Clean My Air Fryer?*

It's recommended to clean your air fryer after each use to prevent the buildup of food residue and grease, which can lead to smoke and unpleasant odors during cooking.

### *3. What's the Best Way to Clean an Air Fryer?*

After every use, remove and clean the basket, pan, and rack with hot water and dish soap. A non-abrasive sponge can be used to scrub off any stuck-on food particles.

Wipe down the inside of the appliance with a damp cloth or sponge.

### *4. Are There Any Foods That Shouldn't Be Cooked in an Air Fryer?*

Foods with wet batter should not be cooked in an air fryer, as they won't crisp up well. Also, delicate foods like lettuce or other leafy greens will likely wilt or burn in an air fryer.

### *5. What Is an Air Fryer And How Does It Work?*

An air fryer is a kitchen appliance that cooks food by circulating hot air around it using the convection mechanism. It creates a crispy layer on the outside of your food, giving it a fried texture without actually deep frying.

### *6. What Types of Foods Can I Cook in an Air Fryer?*

You can cook a variety of foods in an air fryer, including meat, vegetables, frozen foods like fries or nuggets, and even baked goods like cookies or muffins.

### *7. Why Does My Food Come Out Dry When I Use My Air Fryer?*

This could be due to overcooking or not using enough oil. While you don't need much oil for an air fryer compared to traditional frying methods, some is still necessary to prevent drying out.

### *8. Can I Stack Food in My Air Fryer for Cooking More at Once?*

Stacking might cause uneven cooking, as the hot circulating air won't reach all areas evenly. For best results, arrange your food in a single layer with some space between each piece.

### *9. Are There Any Health Benefits Associated With Using an Air Fryer?*

Yes! Because air fryers need less oil than traditional frying methods, you're consuming fewer calories and less fat when you cook with one.

### *10. Does Preheating Make Any Difference When Using an Air Fryer?*

Preheating your air fryer before adding your ingredients can help achieve a crispier finish, especially for certain recipes like French fries or chicken wings.

### *11. How Do I Control Smoke Coming From My Air Fryer?*

If your air fryer is smoking, it might be due to excess oil or food particles left in the pan. Make sure to clean your air fryer thoroughly after each use.

### *12. Can I Use Aluminum Foil or Baking Paper in My Air Fryer?*

Yes, you can, but make sure that it doesn't cover the sides of the basket, and always put food on top of the foil so it won't fly into the heater and start a fire.

### *13. How Do I Achieve the Best Results With My Air Fryer?*

For the best results, avoid overcrowding the basket, use a little bit of oil on your food before cooking, and shake or flip your food halfway through cooking to ensure even crispiness.

### *14. Can I Cook Raw Meat in an Air Fryer?*

Yes, you can! However, it's important to ensure that the meat is cooked thoroughly by using a meat thermometer to check the internal temperatures.

### *15. Do I Need to Preheat My Air Fryer?*

Yes, it's recommended to preheat your air fryer for about 5 minutes before cooking. This helps the food cook more evenly.

### *16. How Much Oil Should I Use in the Air Fryer?*

You only need a small amount of oil, typically 1–2 tablespoons. You can spray or brush the oil onto your food.

### *17. How Do I Prevent Food From Sticking to the Air Fryer Basket?*

To prevent food from sticking, lightly coat the basket with a bit of oil before adding your food.

### *18. How Often Do I Need to Shake or Flip the Food While Cooking?*

For most foods, you should shake or flip them halfway through cooking to ensure even crisping and browning.

### *19. Can I Cook Frozen Foods in an Air Fryer?*

Yes, you can cook frozen foods directly in an air fryer, but it may take slightly longer than fresh foods.

### *20. How Long Does It Take to Cook Food in the Air Fryer?*

Cooking times vary depending on what you're making and how full your basket is, but they generally range from 10 to 25 minutes.

### *21. Can I Bake in an Air Fryer?*

Yes, many models have a baking function and come with a baking pan accessory that fits inside the basket.

### *22. Can I Cook Many Foods at the Same Time?*

Yes, if there's enough space for hot air to circulate around each piece of food for even cooking.

### *23. What Are Common Mistakes to Avoid With an Air Fryer?*

Overcrowding the basket and not using enough oil are two common mistakes that can lead to unevenly cooked results.

### *24. Can I Reheat Food in the Air Fryer?*

Yes, an air fryer can be used to reheat food. It's often faster and results in crispier leftovers than a microwave.

### *25. How Do I Adjust Cooking Times for My Recipes in the Air Fryer?*

Generally, you'll want to reduce both the cooking time and temperature by about 20% from what a traditional oven recipe calls for.

### *26. Can I Make Desserts in an Air Fryer?*

Yes, you can make a variety of desserts, including cakes, cookies, and pastries.

### *27. How Do I Know When the Food Is Done?*

Most foods are done when they've reached a golden-brown color and crispy texture. Use a meat thermometer to check that the meat has reached the recommended internal temperature.

### *28. Can I Cook Without Oil in the Air Fryer?*

While it's possible to cook some food without oil, using a small amount helps achieve the best texture and flavor.

### *29. Can I Use My Air Fryer Like a Microwave?*

No, an air fryer cannot be used as a microwave because it doesn't heat food in the same way. It uses hot air circulation to cook food, which is different from the microwave's method of using radiation.

### *30. Why Isn't My Food as Crispy as Expected?*

This could be due to overcrowding your air fryer or not using enough oil. Ensure you don't overfill your basket and lightly coat your food with oil for crispier results.

### *31. Do I Need to Defrost Food Before Air Frying?*

No, you do not need to defrost frozen foods before putting them in the air fryer, but it may slightly increase cooking time.

### *32. How Long Should I Preheat the Air Fryer?*

Preheating an air fryer usually takes about 5 minutes, but it can vary based on different models.

### *33. Can I Use My Air Fryer for Roasting Vegetables?*

Yes, you can roast vegetables in an air fryer by tossing them in a bit of oil and seasoning, then cooking at high heat until they're tender and browned.

### *34. Do Air Fryers Use a Lot of Electricity?*

Air fryers do consume electricity, but they are more energy-efficient than traditional ovens because they heat up faster and cook food more quickly.

### *35. How Does the Air Fryer Compare to a Convection Oven?*

Air fryers are essentially small countertop convection ovens. They circulate hot air around food, but because they're smaller, they heat up faster and are more energy efficient.

### *36. Can I Make Homemade Fries in the Air Fryer?*

Yes, you can make homemade fries by cutting potatoes into strips, coating them with oil and seasonings, then cooking them until crispy.

### *37. Why Is My Air Fryer Food Soggy?*

Overcrowding or insufficient heating might cause this issue—ensure your food is in a single layer and that the temperature is set high enough.

### *38. How Do I Modify Traditional Oven Recipes for an Air Fryer?*

Most oven recipes can be converted for an air fryer by reducing the cooking temperature by 25 degrees Fahrenheit and cutting down the cooking time by about 20%. However, these conversions may vary depending on the specific recipe ingredients and individual models of air fryers.

### *39. What Kind of Seasoning Should I Use in an Air Fryer?*

You can use any type of seasoning you would normally use in regular frying or baking—from simple salt and pepper to more complex spice blends or marinades.

### *40. Can I Check on Food Midway Through the Cooking Process?*

Yes, in fact, it's recommended to shake the basket halfway through cooking for evenly distributed heat and to check if your food needs more time or if it's done.

### *41. Can Flavors Transfer Between Different Foods When Cooked Together in an Air Fryer?*

Yes, flavors can transfer if you cook different types of food together in an air fryer. To avoid this, it's best to cook different foods separately.

### *42. What Are Some Model-Specific Functions I Should Be Aware of When Using an Air Fryer?*

Some models have preset cooking modes for specific foods like fries, chicken, fish, etc., while others may have features like a "keep warm" function or even dehydrating capabilities. Refer to your model's user manual for detailed information on its specific functions.

### *43. Watch Your Fingers!*

Lastly, exercise caution when removing hot food from the air fryer. The basket and its contents can become very hot, so it's advisable to use oven mitts or a towel to protect your hands. Steam can also escape upon opening the basket, which could cause burns if you're not careful. Treat it with as much caution as you would your oven!

## Wrapping Up

As we wrap up this chapter, I hope you're feeling equipped with a toolkit full of handy solutions to tackle those pesky air fryer hurdles. I think we've covered all the essentials, but don't forget—there's a wealth of air fryer tips, tricks, and information out there, from the internet to your trusty air fryer manual!

I truly hope this frequently asked questions section has given you the confidence to grab your silicone-tipped tongs and dive right into air frying with ease. You've got this!

## Conversion Chart for Common Air Fryer Temperatures in Fahrenheit and Celsius

Here is a comparison list for common air fryer temperatures in Fahrenheit and Celsius:

| Fahrenheit (°F) | Celsius (°C) |
| --- | --- |
| 250°F | 120°C |
| 275°F | 135°C |
| 300°F | 150°C |
| 325°F | 160°C |
| 350°F | 175°C |
| 375°F | 190°C |
| 400°F | 200°C |
| 425°F | 220°C |

These conversions cover typical air fryer settings. Many air fryers use Fahrenheit as the default setting, but the Celsius equivalents are useful for conversions and international recipes.

# Conclusion

Thank you for joining me on this journey through ***The Easy Air Fryer Cookbook With Pictures***. Together, we've unlocked the power of the air fryer, transforming everyday meal prep into an experience that's quick, delicious, and satisfying. Whether you're a busy adult, a health-conscious eater, or a culinary enthusiast, I hope this book has shown you that with the right tools and a touch of creativity, cooking can be both simple and rewarding.

With your air fryer by your side, you can now come home, unwind, and within minutes have a healthy, satisfying meal that doesn't require hours in the kitchen. Meal prep has become an opportunity to experiment, add variety, and put a fresh spin on every dish. Those dinnertime favorites you know and love will never be the same!

I designed this book to be accessible to all, just like my ***Air Fryer Cookbook for Beginners***, providing step-by-step guidance and inspiration for anyone eager to explore air frying. And for those navigating dietary needs, ***The Quick and Easy Gluten-Free Air Fryer Cookbook*** offers another resource to help bring flavorful, easy meals to the table.

Your air fryer is more than an appliance; it's your partner in creating wholesome, budget-friendly meals that support your lifestyle. With lean proteins, vibrant veggies, and a variety of flavors, you're equipped to enjoy delicious, nourishing food every day. Remember, you're encouraged to experiment—let your creativity shine! Try new flavors, combine ingredients, and craft recipes that reflect your unique tastes.

As you continue on this culinary path, remember that each recipe adds to your expertise and confidence. Let your kitchen be a place of exploration, a canvas for your culinary artistry. Share your creations, invite family and friends to join, and turn every meal into a shared experience.

This journey doesn't end here. There's always more to learn, new ingredients to try, and techniques to explore. Let this book serve as a foundation, a springboard into a world of easy, enjoyable cooking that celebrates health, flavor, and simplicity. With your air fryer, newfound skills, and passion for cooking, you're ready to create countless delicious meals and memories in your kitchen.

Here's to scrumptious dishes, happy hearts, and a kitchen filled with joy.

With warm wishes,
Rosa James

# Your Air Fryer Journey Can Inspire Others!

Thank you for bringing ***The Easy Air Fryer Cookbook With Pictures*** into your kitchen. I hope the recipes and tips have made cooking easier, healthier, and more enjoyable for you.

If this book has helped you on your culinary journey, I'd be truly grateful if you could take a moment to leave a review. Your insights can inspire others to discover the versatility of the air fryer, and your experience may offer valuable guidance to those just starting out.

Every story makes a difference—thank you for being part of this one!

With gratitude,
Rosa James x

# Author Bio

**ROSA JAMES**

Rosa James is a culinary maestro, celebrated for her ability to create delicious, flavorful dishes that accommodate a variety of dietary needs. As a working mother with a family of diverse food preferences, she understands the challenge of preparing quick, budget-friendly meals without sacrificing nutrition or taste.

With years of experience and a deep personal connection to food, Rosa shares her expertise in ***The Easy Air Fryer Cookbook With Pictures***. After being diagnosed with celiac disease, she reinvented her cooking style to ensure the book includes recipes for regular, vegetarian, and gluten-free diets. Her journey has resulted in a collection of nutritious, flavorful meals that cater to every palate.

Whether you're new to air frying or an experienced cook seeking fresh ideas, Rosa's book offers solutions for every meal. Her love for desserts also shines through, with indulgent, easy-to-make treats that are just as satisfying as her savory dishes.

Rosa's cookbook is a heartfelt guide for creating simple, nutritious dinners and delightful treats the whole family will love.

# References


*Air fryer maintenance and cleaning.* (2024, April 5). Tru Earth. https://tru.earth/blogs/tru-living/air-fryer-maintenance-and-cleaning

*Benefits of cooking with an air fryer.* (2023, September 28). Taurus; Taurus. https://taurus-home.com/en/blogs/blog-taurus/benefits-of-cooking-with-an-air-fryer?srsltid=AfmBOorC5AmL65TxlEQDT3mAOueW35wVudesl4DCQxCnWHOuBpy8avSY

Curry, K. (2023, July 20). *How healthy are they? Are there air fryer benefits?* Fit Men Cook. https://fitmencook.com/blog/air-fryer-benefits/

*Different types of air fryers.* (n.d.). Innoteck. Retrieved August 1, 2024, from https://innoteck.co.uk/different-types-of-air-fryers/

Farris, E. (2023, June 9). *How to use your convection oven as an air fryer.* Epicurious. https://www.epicurious.com/shopping/how-to-use-your-convection-oven-as-an-air-fryer

Foster, K. (2015). *10 common mistakes that every cook makes.* Kitchn. https://www.thekitchn.com/10-common-mistakes-that-every-cook-makes-mistakes-in-the-kitchen-217949

*Guide to air frying in a convection oven.* (n.d.). KitchenAid. https://www.kitchenaid.com/pinch-of-help/major-appliances/air-frying-in-convection-oven.html

*How to choose an air fryer.* (n.d.). Blue Jean Chef. https://bluejeanchef.com/cooking-school/how-to-choose-an-air-fryer/

*How to use an air fryer for perfectly crispy results.* (2024). Instacart. https://www.instacart.com/company/ideas/how-to-use-an-air-fryer-in-5-easy-steps/

Kabir, S. R. (2023, December 21). *Who invented the air fryer? Full story of the magic appliance.* History Cooperative. https://historycooperative.org/who-invented-the-air-fryer/

Kring, L. (2023). *21 common cooking mistakes and how to avoid them.* Foodal. https://foodal.com/knowledge/how-to/common-cooking-mistakes/

*Mistakes most people make with their air fryer.* (2023, April 3). Air Fryer Papi. https://airfryerpapi.com/mistakes-most-people-make-with-their-air-fryer/#google_vignette

Nawab, A. (2024, August 29). *Tips for cleaning and maintaining air fryers.* Haier India. https://shop.haierindia.com/blog/air-fryer-maintenance-tips-longevity/?srsltid=AfmBOoqdx6L1jIsZFGcusw-Y-LG0DSZv4KGvKjsyHbw8tqNWb67GM4qj

Reeves, E. (2022). *6 reasons why you need an air fryer in your kitchen.* B&Q. https://www.diy.com/ideas--advice/kitchen/appliances/6-reasons-why-you-need-an-air-fryer-in-your-kitchen

Shoes, J. (2022). *5 benefits of an air fryer: Why you need one.* John's Shoe and Accessories. https://www.johnshoes.com/blog/post/5-benefits-of-an-air-fryer-why-you-need-one.html

Silvia, P. (2023, January 30). *Air fry vs. convection: Which oven setting is better?* Colders. https://www.colders.com/blog/air-fry-vs-convection

Watsky, D. (2024). *A complete guide to air fryers: Everyone's new favorite kitchen appliance.* CNET. https://www.cnet.com/home/kitchen-and-household/a-complete-guide-to-air-fryers-everyones-new-favorite-kitchen-appliance/

*What are the different types of air fryers?* (n.d.). Innoteck. Retrieved August 1, 2024, from https://innoteck.co.uk/what-are-the-different-types-of-air-fryers/

## Image References

Images provided by author.

Made in United States
Cleveland, OH
26 March 2025